HELLO CELLO POSITIONS!

4th Position Book

By Jisoo Ok

for Young Cellists

First edition July 2020

ISBN 978-1-7350859-2-0

www.hellocellobooks.com

Publications by Jisoo Ok:

Hello Cello Positions! Second Position
Hello Cello Positions! Third Position
Hello Cello Positions! Fourth Position

Available at amazon.com

Author's Note

While experienced cellists have developed a firm understanding of the importance of navigating the fingerboard through years of training, beginners, especially young students, often struggle with the process of learning and understanding fingerboard positions.

Despite years of searching for the right guide to teach the neck positions, I was unable to find a suitable book designed for young cellists that explained the positions in a comprehensive, yet fun and easy-to-understand, manner.

It is through my passion to help my cello students learn the positions in a simple and fun way that this book was born.

I would like to thank my amazing students, Emma, Alyssa, Juliet, Darcy and Aarika, for inspiring me to write this book! Thanks to Agnes Kwasniewska for introducing me to these wonderful students at the Virtuoso Suzuki Academy.

I am eternally grateful to all my former cello teachers - Kim Young-Suk, James Tennant, Natalia Pavlutskaya, Fred Sherry and Bonnie Hampton. I am thankful to Pamela Devenport for teaching Suzuki philosophies and methods of cello teaching with a unique and masterful approach.

Special thanks to my cousin, Isabel Kwon, a Juilliard trained cellist, for her advice and insights and to my brother-in-law John Ahn for helping me with editing and proofreading. Finally, to my family, my husband Hector, my son Santiago, my sister Krystal, and my parents for their love and support.

I had so much fun composing and arranging the pieces in this book!
I hope you have as much fun learning and playing them!

Enjoy!
Jisoo Ok

Content

Hello Backward Extended Fourth Position on C string!

Hello Upper Fourth Position   24

Hello Forward Extended Fourth Position

4th Position Review Party!

Final Review Party!

Cello Map

Closed Hand Position
Half steps between each fingers

C G D A

C#	G#	Eb	Bb	1/2 postion
D	A	E	B	1st position
Eb	Bb	F	C	Lower 2nd position
E	B	F#	C#	Upper 2nd position
F	C	G	D	3rd position (Lower 3rd position)
F#	C#	G#	Eb	Upper 3rd position
G	D	A	E	4th position
Ab	Eb	Bb	F	Upper 4th position
A	E	B	F#	
Bb	F	C	G	
B	F#	C#	G#	

Common Enharmonic Notes
(Different names for the same note)
C# = Db
D# = Eb
F# = Gb
G# = Ab
A# = Bb

Fourth Positions

4th Position

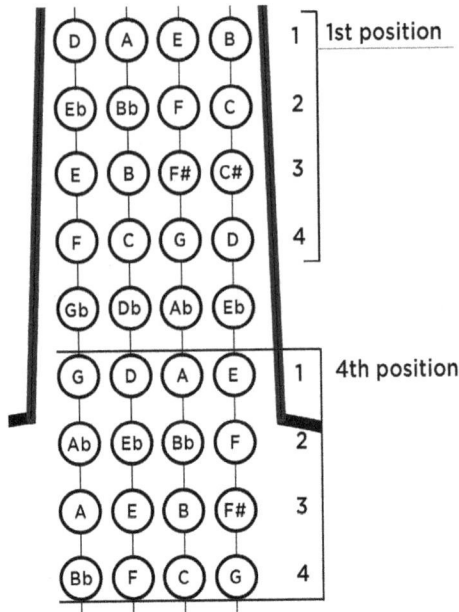

Backward Extended 4th Position

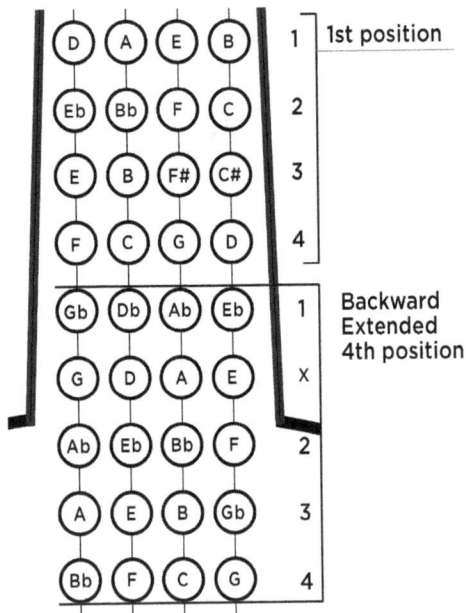

Upper 4th Position

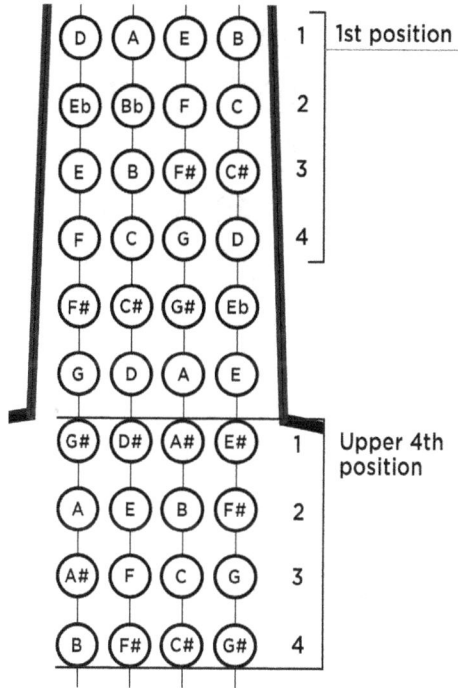

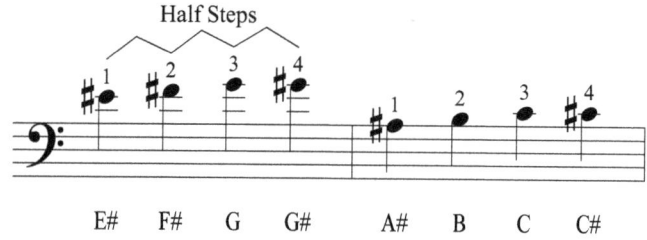

Forward Extended 4th Position

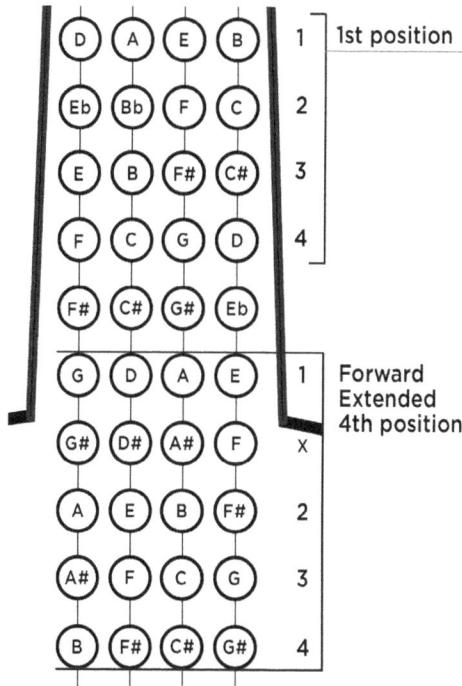

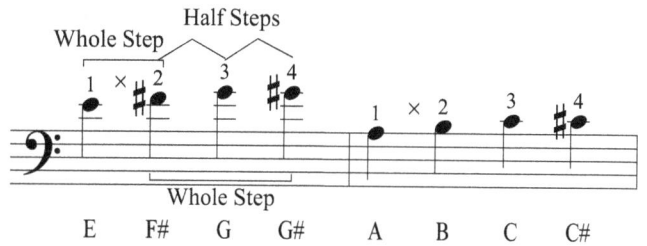

Hello 4th Position on A string!

4th Position

4   1   2   #3   4

0

G   G   G   E   F   F#   G

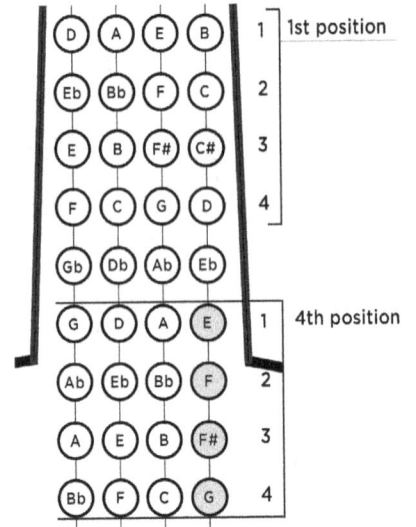

Hey There!

Octave Apart

Let's name the notes!

Going Up and Down

Distant Echo

Ice Skating

Hello 4th Positon on D string!

4th Position

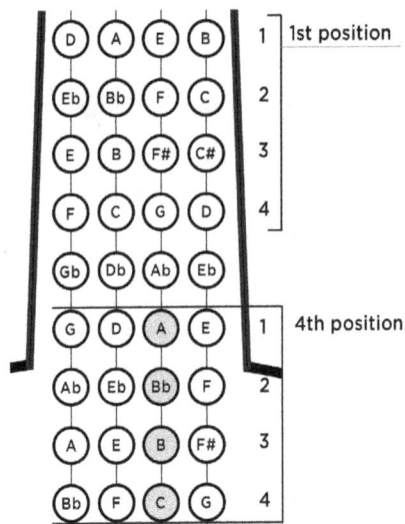

1st position

4th position

A A A Bb B C

Hey There!

Octave Apart

Let's name the notes!

Going Up and Down

Sleepy Sloth

Road Trip

8

A Mysterious Cave

Dancing Panda Bear

Purerehua
Butterfly Song

Maori Folk Song

Hush Little Baby

Traditional American

Hello 4th Position on G string!

Hey There!

Octave Apart

Let's name the notes!

Going Up and Down

Easy Peasy Lemon Squeezy

Ice Skating

Hello 4th Position on C string!

4th Position

0   1   1   2   3   4

G   G   G   A♭   A   B♭

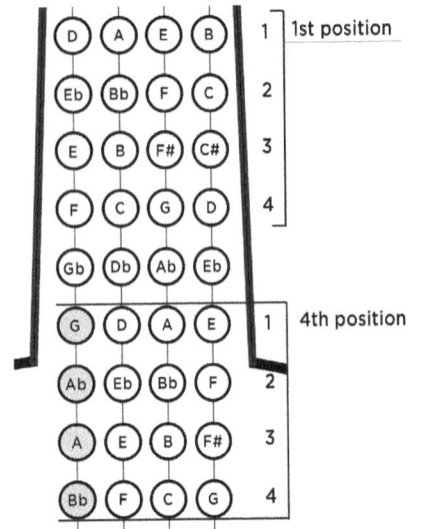

Hey There!

Unison Apart

G string   C string   G string   C string

Let's name the notes!

Going Up and Down

Lazy Cat

Aura Lee

George R. Poulton
(1828-1867)

Elephant in the Circus

Skippy, the Baby Kangaroo

Pop Goes the Weasel

Traditional

Swan Lake

Pyotr Ilyich Tchaikovsky
(1840-1893)

16

Hello Backward Extended 4th Position on A string!

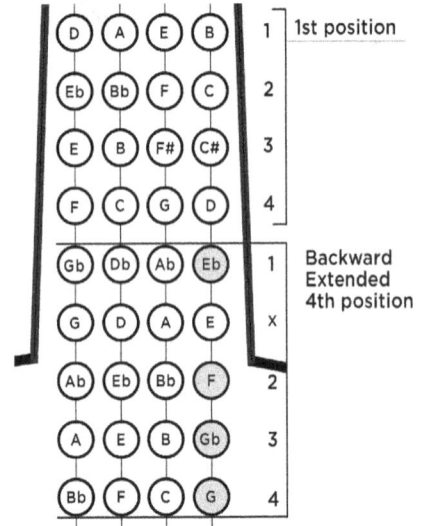

Backward Extended 4th Position

G　　G　　G　　　E♭　F　G♭　G

Hot Cross Buns

Traditional

Au Clair de la Lune

French Folk Song

Downstairs & Upstairs at Aunt Rhody's

Let's name the notes!

A Short Hike

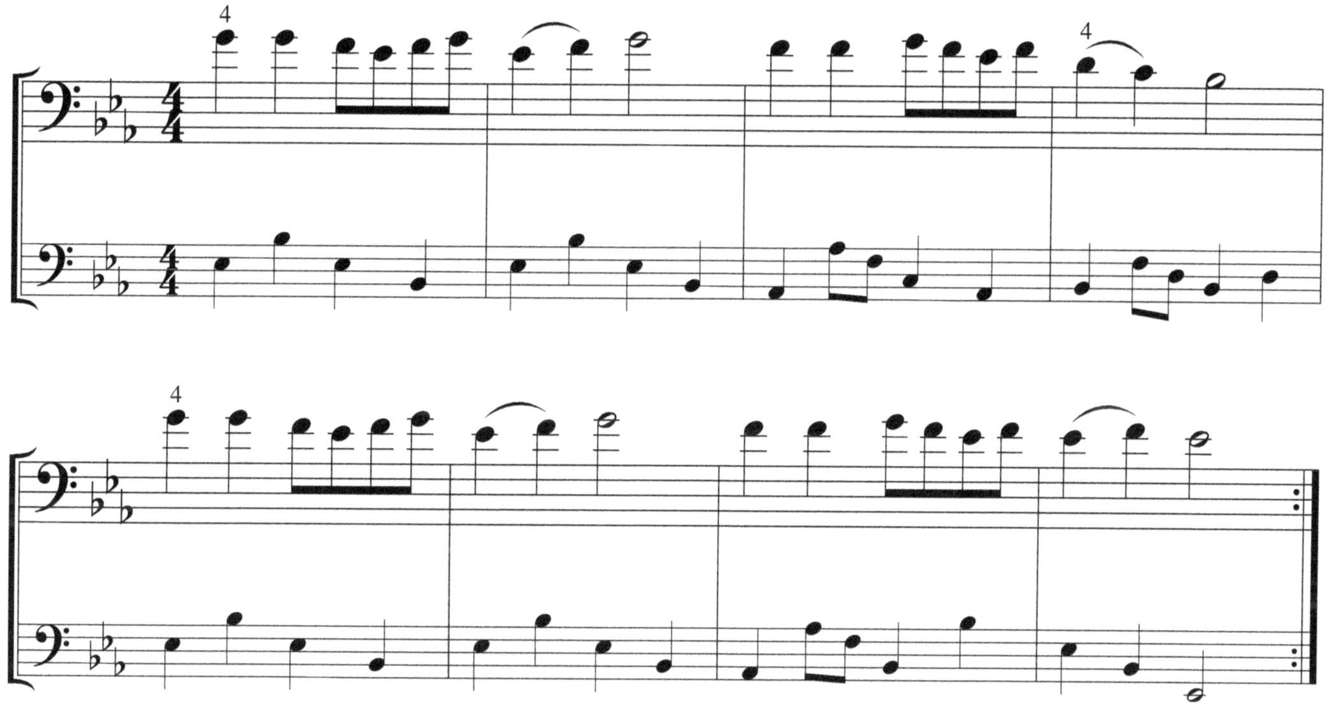

Los Pollitos

Mexican Folk Song

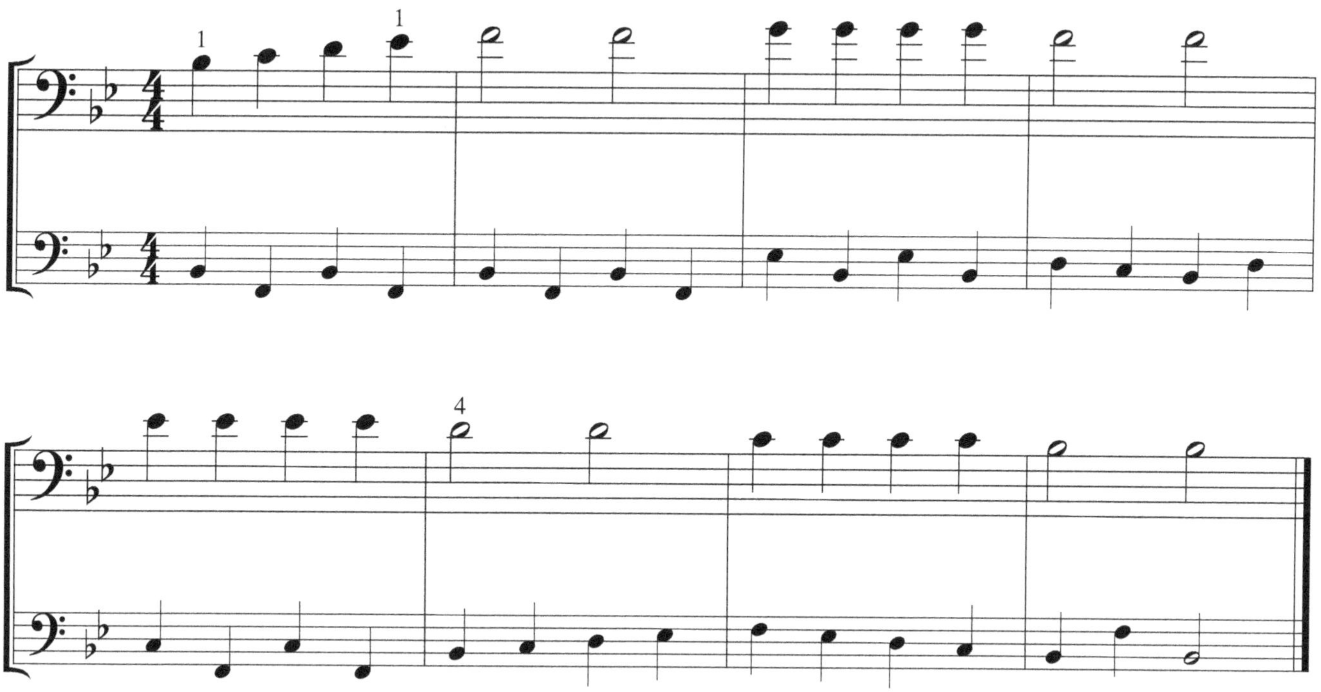

Hello Backward Extended 4th Position on D string!

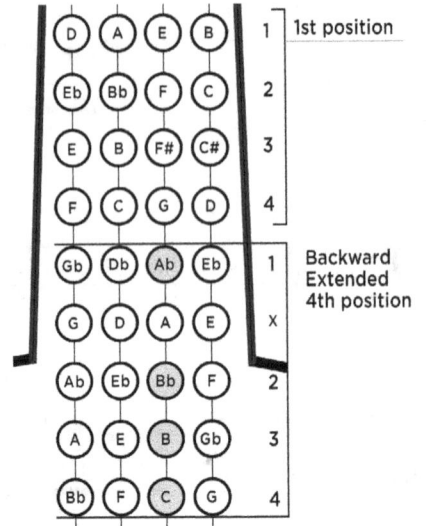

Backward Extended 4th Position

C   C   C   Ab   Bb   B   C

D	A	E	B	1	1st position
Eb	Bb	F	C	2	
E	B	F#	C#	3	
F	C	G	D	4	
Gb	Db	Ab	Eb	1	Backward Extended 4th position
G	D	A	E	X	
Ab	Eb	Bb	F	2	
A	E	B	Gb	3	
Bb	F	C	G	4	

Hot Cross Buns

Traditional

Au Clair de la Lune

French Folk song

Downstairs & Upstairs at Aunt Rhody's

— — — —   — — — —   — — — —

Let's name the notes!

Dancing Polar Bear

Morning
from Peer Gynt

Edvard Grieg
(1843-1907)

Hello Backward Extended 4th Position on G string!

Backward Extended 4th Position

F   F   D♭   E♭   E   F

Hot Cross Buns

Traditional

Au Clair de la Lune

French Folk Song

Downstairs & Upstairs at Auntie Rhody's

Let's name the notes!

Are We There Yet?

The Muffin Man

Traditional

Hello Backward Extended 4th Position on C string!

Backward Extended 4th Position

B♭   B♭   G♭   A♭   A   B♭

	D	A	E	B	1	1st position
	Eb	Bb	F	C	2	
	E	B	F#	C#	3	
	F	C	G	D	4	
	Gb	Db	Ab	Eb	1	Backward Extended 4th position
	G	D	A	E	X	
	Ab	Eb	Bb	F	2	
	A	E	B	Gb	3	
	Bb	F	C	G	4	

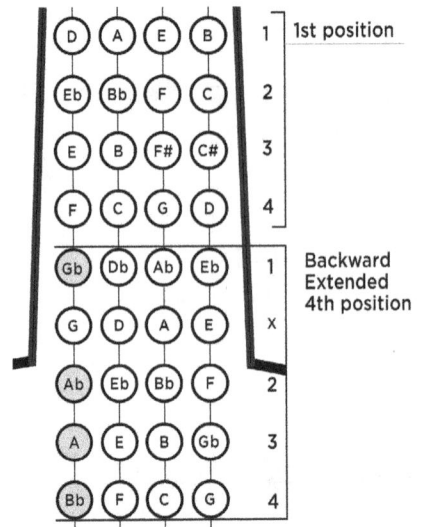

Hot Cross Buns

Traditional

Au Clair de la Lune

French Folk Song

Don't Tell Aunt Rhody

Let's name the notes!

Naturals vs. Flats

Lions in the Circus

Hello Upper 4th Position!

Upper 4th Position

Same four notes with different names

G G G   E# F# G G#   F Gb G Ab

Upper 4th Position

C C C   A# B C C#   Bb B C Db

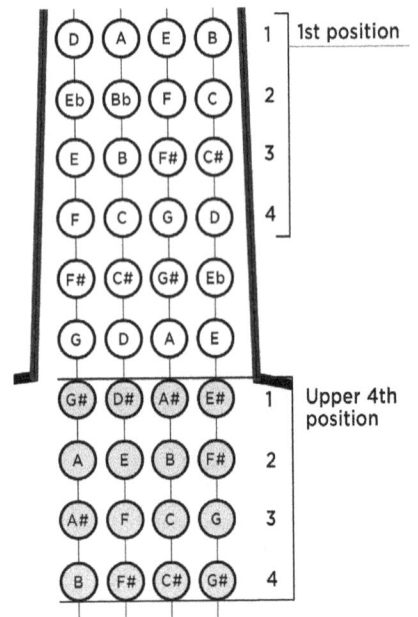

Upper 4th Position

F F F   D# E F F#   Eb E F Gb

Same Position with Different Names

Upper 4th Position

A# A# A#   G# A A# B   Ab A B Cb

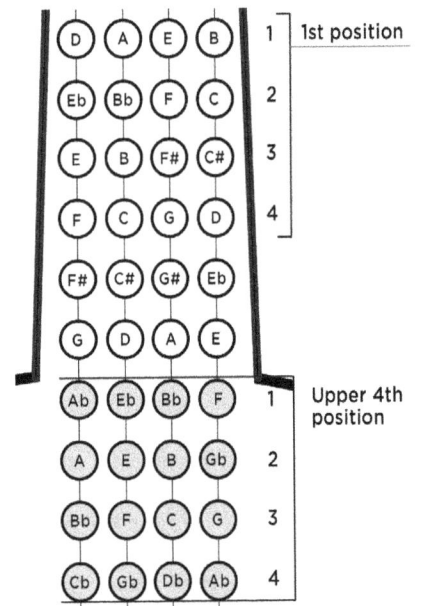

Short Etude
from Practical Method Op. 12

Josef Werner

Lazy Cat

Dancing Panda Bear

* Try playing Dancing Panda and Little Goose in the upper 4th position & the half position.

Little Goose

Same but Different
Upper 4th and Half Positions

Skippy, the Baby Kangaroo

28

Hello Forward Extended 4th Position!

E F# G G#   A B C C#

D E F F#   G A A# B

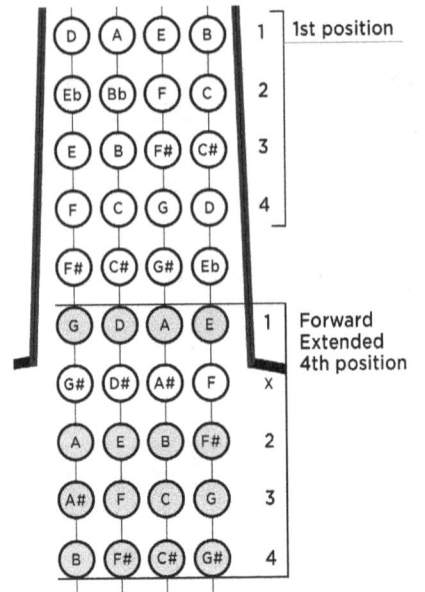

Mary Had a Little Lamb

Traditional

Au Clair de la Lune

French Folk Song

Downstairs & Upstairs at Aunt Rhodie's

Climbing Up to the Tree House

Hot Cross Buns

Squire's Tarantella Sneak Peak

Silly Goose

A sharp vs. A natural

Morning
from Peer Gynt

Edvard Grieg
(1843-1907)

Dancing Polar Bear

4th Position Review Party!

Home on the Range

Daniel E. Kelley
(1843-1905)

The Drunken Sailor

Traditional

The Skater's Waltz

Emile Waldteufel
(1837-1915)

Arirang

Korean Folk Song

Auld Lang Syne

Scottish Folk Song

36

Final Reveiw Party!

Londonderry Air

Irish Folk Song

Lullaby

Johannes Brahms
(1833-1897)

Allegro Maestoso
from Water Music

George Handel
(1685–1759)

Santa Lucia

Neapolitan Folk Song

Gavotte
from English Suite No. 3

Johann Sebastian Bach
(1685-1750)

El Choclo

Ángel Villoldo
(1861-1919)

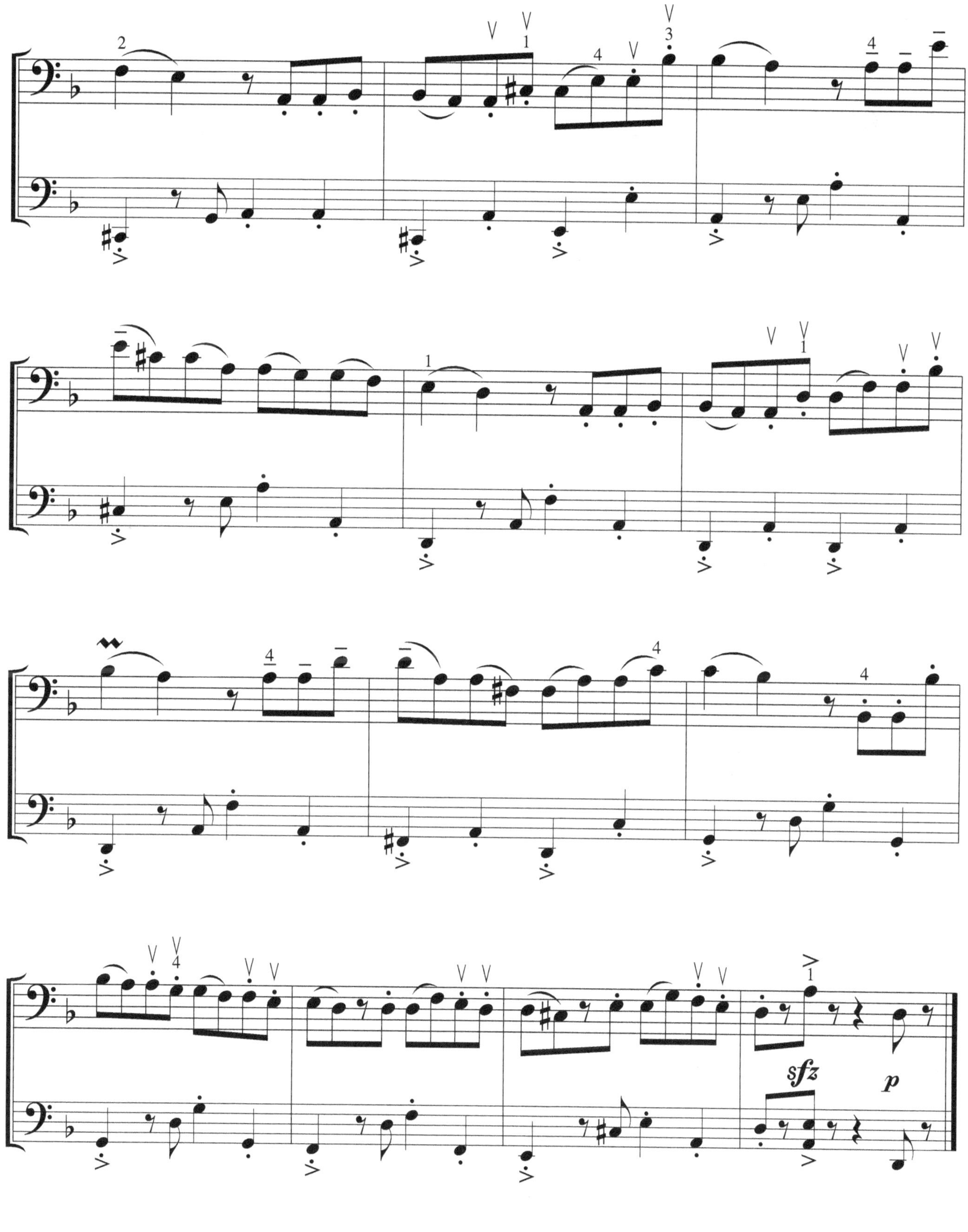
sfz
p

Spring Song
Song without Words, Op. 62 No. 6

Felix Mendelssohn
(1809-1847)

Theme
from Marriage of Figaro

Wolfgang Amadeus Mozart
(1756-1791)

Pomp and Circumstance

Edward Elgar
(1857-1934)

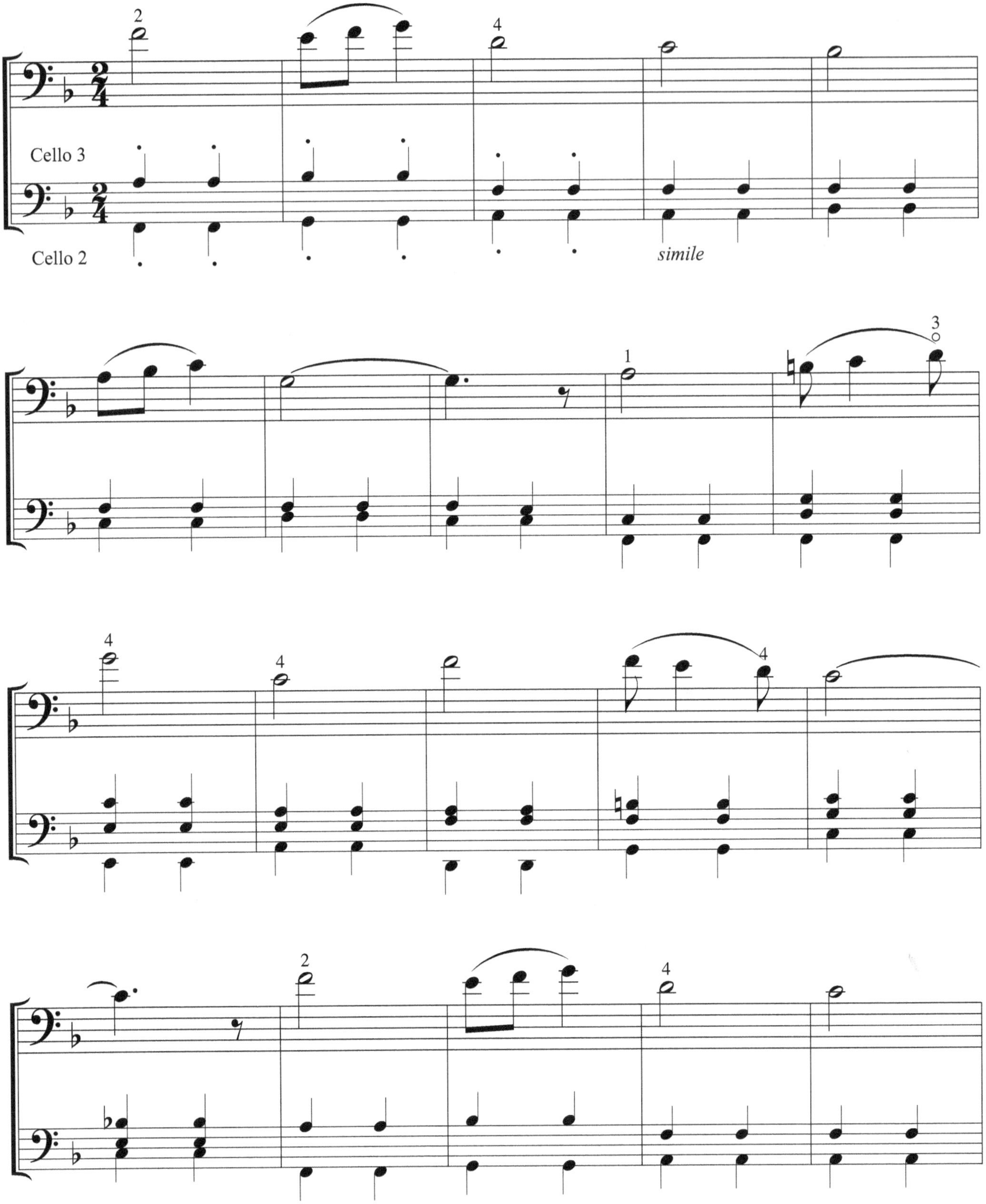

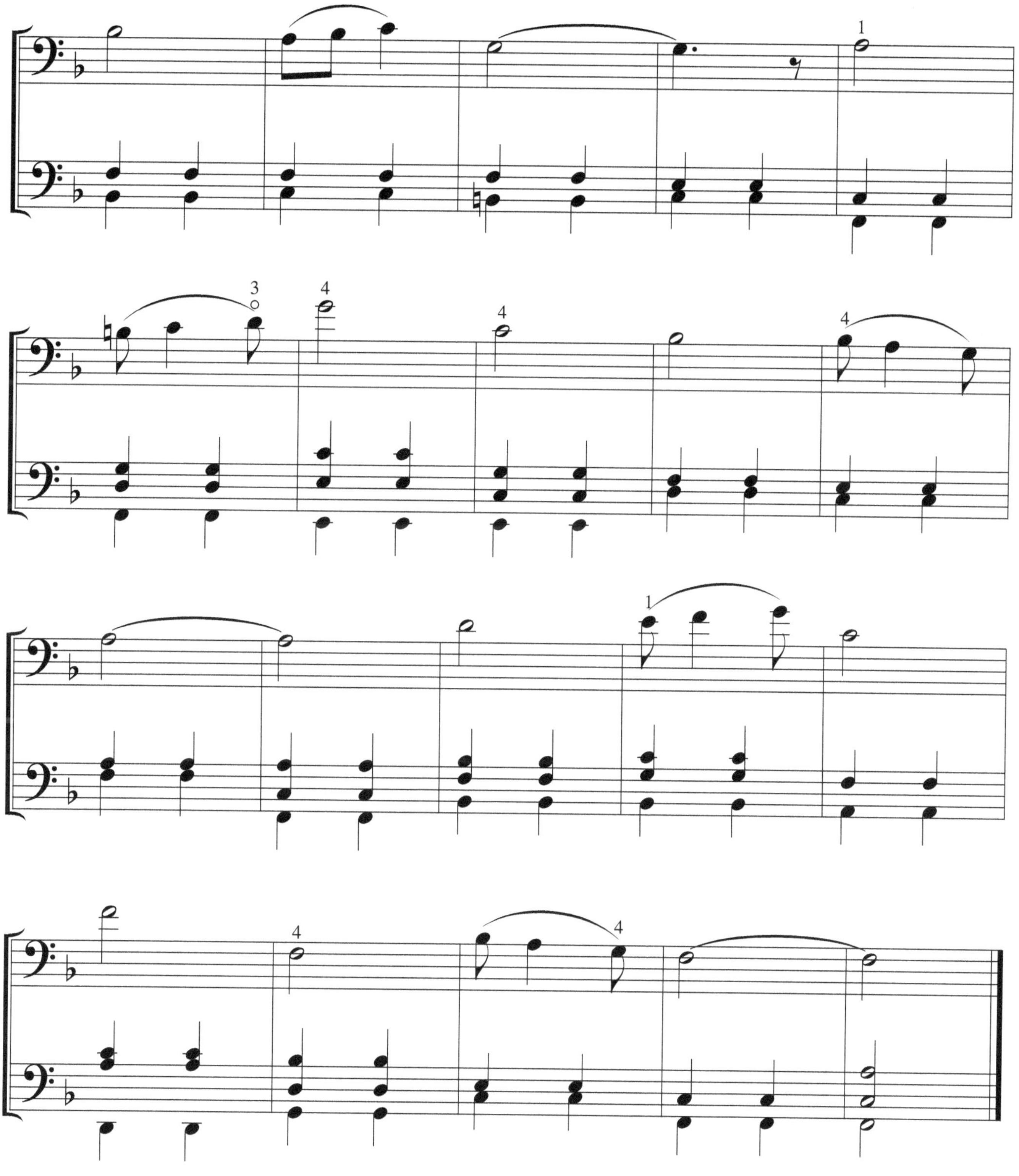

About the Author

As a Latin Grammy nominee, **Jisoo Ok** enjoys a multi-faceted and vibrant musical career as a cellist, festival director, arranger, orchestrator, recording artist and educator of classical and tango music.

Jisoo is deeply committed to exploring connections with musicians from other backgrounds and disciplines. This deep commitment can be seen in her collaborations with distinguished artists, such as latin jazz clarinetist Paquito D'Rivera, tango pianist Pablo Ziegler, bandoneonist Hector Del Curto, jazz violinist Regina Carter and bassist Ron Carter.

She has performed at prestigious venues and festivals, such as Carnegie Hall, Aspen Music Festival, La Jolla Music SummerFest, the Chautauqua Institute, Mondavi Center for the Performing Arts, Blue Note and National Concert Hall in Taiwan. As a soloist, she has performed with Rochester Philharmonic Orchestra and Lancaster Symphony Orchestra.

Her arrangements, orchestrations and transcriptions have been performed by top orchestras, such as Rochester Philharmonic Orchestra, St. Louis Symphony, Vermont Symphony Orchestra, Lancaster Symphony Orchestra, Billings Symphony Orchestra, Aspen Music Festival Chamber Orchestra and Stowe Tango Music Festival Orchestra.

Jisoo's dedication as a teacher can be seen in the success of her cello students, who have won numerous competitions and were accepted to Manhattan School of Music, New England Conservatory, Indiana University, The Juilliard School Pre-College, All-National Honors Orchestra and All-New York State Orchestra. She teaches privately and at the Virtuoso Suzuki Academy in Long Island, NY.

Jisoo was born in Seoul, Korea and raised in New Zealand. She has participated in master classes with Janos Starker, Bernard Greenhouse, Paul Katz, Laurence Lesser and Anner Bylsma. She received her Bachelor's and Master's degrees from The Juilliard School, studying with Bonnie Hampton and Fred Sherry. She studied chamber music with Itzhak Perlman and Robert Mann.

She is the co-founder and co- director of the Stowe Tango Music Festival, the premier tango music festival in the United States.

www.okcellist.com